Vietnam War

Library of Congress Cataloging-in-Publication Data

Hills, Ken.
    Vietnam War / by Ken Hills : illustrated by Andrew Howat.
    Library ed.
        p. cm. — (Wars that changed the world)
    Includes index.
    Summary: Surveys the history of the conflict in Vietnam, from its
involvement in France's colonial empire to the union of North and
South Vietnam as a single communist nation after the withdrawal of
American troops
    ISBN 1-85435-259-8
    1. Vietnamese Conflict, 1961-1975 Juvenile literature.
(1. Vietnamese Conflict, 1961-1975.) I. Howat, Andrew, ill.
II. Title. III. Series.
DS567.7.H55 1991
909.07 – dc20

                                            90-25395
                                            CIP
                                            AC

Library Edition Published 1991

Published by Marshall Cavendish Corporation
2415 Jerusalem Avenue
PO Box 587, North Bellmore,
N.Y. 11710

Library edition produced by Pemberton Press
Printed by New Interlitho, Milan

Designed and produced by
AS Publishing

WARS THAT CHANGED THE WORLD

Vietnam War

By Ken Hills
Illustrated by Andrew Howat

MARSHALL CAVENDISH
NEW YORK · LONDON · TORONTO · SYDNEY

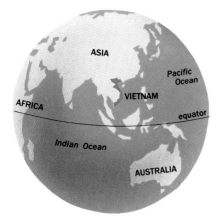

Above: Vietnam is a tiny tropical country in Southeast Asia.

Below: The Vietnamese are farmers. Their main food is rice which they grow in fertile paddy fields in the two great river deltas.

Vietnam: Land and People

The Vietnamese people have been at war for most of their history. Their small country is part of Indochina and Southeast Asia. Long ago their neighbors to the north, the Chinese, conquered their homeland, the area that is now Vietnam. For centuries not only the Chinese but also European colonists fought over the country.

Colonial Life

By the end of the 19th century Vietnam and the rest of Indochina had become part of France's colonial empire. The French ruled Indochina from Hanoi, the capital city of Vietnam. They built roads and railroads so that they could export the sugar and rice that the peasant farmers grew. But the people benefited little. They remained poor and were excluded from any part in government. Most of them lived simply, in small villages in the fertile lowlands along the coast, or in the swampy deltas of

Vietnam's two great rivers, the Red and the Mekong.

Discontent with their rulers turned to revolt. After eight years of struggle the Vietnamese threw the French out. They were led by Ho Chi Minh, who was a Communist. His political beliefs were shared by many Vietnamese but also opposed by many. As a result the country was divided. The north of the country became North Vietnam, a Communist state ruled by Ho Chi Minh. The south became South Vietnam, an anti-Communist state led by Ngo Dinh Diem.

Peace did not last long. Communists in South Vietnam, with help from North Vietnam, began to undermine Diem's government. By 1959 war had broken out – not just a civil war but a war that involved the world's greatest nations and at times seemed to threaten the whole world.

The Defeat of the French

France had ruled Indochina since the late 1800s. During World War II (1941-45), the Japanese occupied Indochina. In 1945, after the final defeat of Japan, the French hastened to regain control of their former colony. But they did not move as fast as Ho Chi Minh. He slipped across the Chinese border and set up a government in Hanoi.

The French rapidly built up their forces. Surprisingly, they agreed to recognize Ho's government in the north, but it was an uneasy compromise. Neither side kept its promises, and fighting soon broke out between them.

Giap's Guerrillas

The Vietnamese forces in the north were called the Vietminh. They were led by Ho's long-time comrade Vo Nguyen Giap. Together they had learned the theories of revolution and guerrilla warfare developed by the Chinese Communist leader, Mao Tse-Tung. Following Mao's example, Giap avoided open warfare and used small bands of men, often by night, to attack the French where they were weak and unprepared. Soon the French were safe only in the main cities. Outside, in the jungles and rice fields, the Vietminh controlled the land. They were well equipped with arms and supplies from Communist China.

By 1954, the French people wanted to get out of the war. It was hugely expensive, in money and lives. General Henri Navarre, the French commander, realized that he had to win the war quickly or the French cause was doomed.

Dien Bien Phu

Navarre planned to lure the main Vietminh force out of hiding to fight a battle at a place where it would be

HO CHI MINH

Born Nguyen Van Thanh in Vietnam in 1890, Ho Chi Minh became a Communist in 1920 and helped found the French Communist Party. As a young man, he traveled in Europe and China, studying the tactics of revolution. Forced to live in exile, he plotted to overthrow the French in his native land. Ho never commanded armies in battle, but he was the guiding spirit of his people. He continued to spur them to victory until his death in 1969. His people loved him and called him "Uncle Ho." When Saigon, the capital of South Vietnam, was eventually conquered, the people renamed it Ho Chi Minh City after him.

destroyed by superior French weapons and firepower. He chose Dien Bien Phu, a small village in a valley, on a vital road through the mountains of northern Vietnam. The Vietminh had no air force, so Navarre thought it safe to supply his forces by air. His plan went badly wrong.

The Vietminh hauled guns over mountain tracks the French thought were impassable. These guns ringed the defenses and bombarded the landing strips, making them unusable. When the Vietminh brought up antiaircraft guns, even dropping men and supplies by parachute became impossible. The French were cut off. On May 7, 1954, they gave in. French rule in Vietnam was over.

French aircraft and paratroops were easy targets for the Vietminh guns. The French thought that their 16,000-strong garrison at Dien Bien Phu was indestructible, but it was totally overwhelmed by the 50,000 men amassed by General Giap.

America Drifts to War

A conference at Geneva formally ended French rule and created the two rival states. North of the border was Ho's regime, committed to uniting the country under Communist rule. On the other side was South Vietnam, a state founded to oppose Communism.

The Viet Cong

South Vietnam was soon in trouble. The government of Ngo Dinh Diem was detested, and the South Vietnamese army was poorly trained and badly led. There were plenty of recruits to the Viet Cong, a Communist rebel force. Thousands of North Vietnamese, trained in sabotage and guerrilla warfare, poured into the South, followed by units of the North Vietnamese Army.

By the early 1960s, the Viet Cong had seized control of huge areas of South Vietnam. President Diem waged a ruthless and savage campaign against his opponents, but this served only to turn more people against him.

From the United States, newly elected President John F. Kennedy sent more American advisers and arms. But the chaos in the South grew worse. President Diem and his family were murdered in a plot hatched by the army. A series of incompetent military regimes followed.

United States Forces Move in

President Kennedy was assassinated in 1963. His successor, Lyndon B. Johnson, was no less committed to preventing South Vietnam from falling into Communist hands. By 1964 the North Vietnamese army was fighting openly in South Vietnam, and the South Vietnamese forces were doing little to prevent them.

Right: President John F. Kennedy, who ordered the first big buildup of American military power in Vietnam.

Below: Landed by sea, U.S. Marines wade ashore. Their task is to protect the huge American base at Da Nang, not far from the border.

In August 1964, North Vietnamese torpedo boats reportedly attacked American destroyers in the Gulf of Tonkin. American public opinion was outraged. Encouraged by the U.S. Congress, President Johnson ordered a massive build-up of military power in South Vietnam. More military advisers were moved in, and U.S. Army helicopters flew combat missions against the North Vietnamese and the Viet Cong.

Early in 1965 the Viet Cong attacked an American barracks near Saigon and killed or wounded many troops. The Americans struck back quickly. On February 7, President Johnson ordered the U.S. Air Force to bomb military targets across the border in North Vietnam itself. The war was now an international conflict.

At times, six carriers from the U.S. Seventh Fleet were operating off the coast of Vietnam. Carrier aircraft virtually destroyed North Vietnam's main port, Haiphong.

U.S. Base: Vietnam

The United States took over control of the war. Conscription (compulsory military service) was reintroduced in America for the first time since the Korean War ended in the 1950s. Young men were drafted from civilian life and, after brief training, sent to fight in faraway Vietnam.

By June 1966 there were 265,000 American troops in South Vietnam, with more on the way. The United States had the world's second biggest navy, the largest air force and an army equipped with the most advanced weapons. With this might, America turned South Vietnam into one huge military base.

The United States was determined to halt the spread of Communism. Like previous presidents, Johnson believed that the nations of Southeast Asia were particularly vulnerable to Communist aggression. If one nation fell to the Communists, the others would fall, too, one by one, like a row of dominoes.

America's Hopes

The United States came to Vietnam confident that its military might would swiftly destroy all opposition. America's vast wealth and the power of her industry meant that there were almost limitless resources available. The Americans set up huge bases. Their fleet patrolled the waters off the coast, cutting off all supplies that might have come to their enemy by sea. Aircraft carriers stationed in the South China Sea provided safe landing for aircraft close to the battlegrounds. Long-range heavy bombers, based on islands in the Pacific, could mount massive bombing raids on the North.

A Viet Cong, or VC, guerrilla. American soldiers called the VC "Charlie." Their saying was "the night belongs to Charlie."

Day and Night

American troops became a familiar sight to the South Vietnamese in Saigon and other major cities. People in the villages grew accustomed to them landing in their helicopters and patrolling the countryside by day. They looked as if they were in charge. But by night, it was a different story.

After dark the Americans returned to the lights of the cities or shut themselves up in their bunkers behind the barbed wire that surrounded their bases. It was then that the Viet Cong guerrillas slipped silently out of hiding. They moved stealthily along hidden trails through the jungles and paddy fields.

A trip wire that detonated a grenade was one of many deadly booby traps that awaited the Americans in the jungle.

General Giap was the Communists' military genius. With his friend Ho Chi Minh, he learned the basics of guerrilla warfare from the Chinese leader Mao Tse-Tung.

Guerrilla War

Years of fighting the French had made General Giap a brilliant guerrilla commander. His Viet Cong guerrillas had undermined the South Vietnamese government and won control of the countryside. They ruled the civilian population – by terror. They tortured and murdered anyone whom they suspected of opposing them. Families and even whole communities were killed to frighten the rest into obedience.

The Elusive Enemy

The Americans were isolated in their bases. The jungles and rice fields surrounding them were Viet Cong territory,

Another nightmarish hazard to American troops were camouflaged pits studded with sharpened bamboo stakes smeared with poison.

littered with booby traps designed to maim or kill.

It was impossible for the U.S. troops to tell who was Viet Cong and who was not. The guerrillas looked and talked like anyone else. Viet Cong tactics were to hit and run. By the time the Americans responded, the guerrillas had melted into the jungle or assumed the appearance of harmless civilians going about their business.

Much of the ground fighting took place in the jungle, which gave the guerrillas a great advantage. To the Americans the jungle was a strange and frightening place. To the Viet Cong it was home. Many times U.S. troops fought fierce actions in the jungle and had men killed and wounded without seeing a single enemy. Such warfare sapped their morale and wore down their resistance.

TUNNEL SYSTEMS

The Viet Cong dug elaborate tunnel systems that stretched for miles below the jungle floor. Some were dug as bomb shelters. Others were huge strongholds where hundreds of armed soldiers could live underground for weeks on end. The tunnels were well hidden. Many times, when the Americans thought they had cleared an area, the Viet Cong would slip out of their tunnels by night and create havoc in the rear.

SMART BOMBS

The U.S. tried the latest military technology to hit small targets. The "Smart bomb" had a guidance system. It homed onto a reflected laser beam shone at the target by another aircraft. Smart bombs could demolish a key railroad bridge at the first attempt.

Opposite: B-52 bombers were key weapons in Operation Rolling Thunder. Originally designed as long-range nuclear bombers, they were modified to carry high explosives. A single B-52D could carry 102 bombs, weighing over 27 tons, on a 12-hour round trip from the Pacific island of Guam.

"Rolling Thunder"

The aim of the United States was to force North Vietnam to stop fighting, but avoid losing men in ground combat. They decided to bomb the enemy into withdrawal.

General William Westmoreland, the American forces commander in Southeast Asia, planned a bombing campaign code-named "Rolling Thunder." He thought that a few short, sharp attacks would hurt the North Vietnamese enough to make them stop the war and withdraw from the South. He was mistaken.

The North Vietnamese and their Viet Cong allies shrugged off the damage caused by the early raids, and carried on fighting. The Americans replied with heavier and more frequent bombing. Roads, railroads and bridges leading to the South became prime targets. In North Vietnam itself, factories, harbors, and whole cities were destroyed. But still the Communists fought on.

The U.S. Air Force did not have it all their own way in the skies over Vietnam. As the battle developed, Soviet-built MiG fighters, flown by Soviet-trained North Vietnamese pilots, rose to challenge the American planes. But they were never a major threat. Chinese antiaircraft batteries, installed to defend key targets, and surface-to-air missiles caused more serious U.S. losses.

Calling off the Thunder

By December 1967, Operation Rolling Thunder had poured nearly 900,000 tons of bombs on North Vietnam. Casualties must have been horrendous, but the North Vietnamese showed no sign of giving in. American public opinion saw that the bombing had failed to end the war. Peace had to be sought at the conference table.

War in the Jungle

Between 1965 and 1971, U.S. planes dropped over two million tons of bombs on the jungles of Indochina. Their chief target was a spider's web of tracks weaving through dense jungles, over high mountain passes and across wide rivers – the Ho Chi Minh Trail.

Communist Lifeline

Ho Chi Minh had ordered the trail to be made in 1959. From North Vietnam it ran south following the South Vietnamese border, but for its whole length it lay safely in the territory of neutral neighbors Laos and Cambodia. The Communists believed, correctly, that the United States would not attack the trail with its ground forces. Opinion inside and outside the United States would have been outraged by any incursion into neutral countries.

Tracks led from the trail itself across the border into South Vietnam. Along them, usually by night, passed a steady stream of men and equipment to reinforce and supply the Communists. In 1968 alone, 100,000 troops traveled along the trail. Originally the surface of the tracks was beaten earth, suitable for use only by people on foot or bicycle. Gradually it was improved as all-weather roads and new bridges were built to take heavy trucks, tanks, and artillery. An oil pipeline was constructed alongside the road to fuel the growing traffic.

The bombing devastated vast areas of countryside and created massive refugee problems as survivors living near the trail fled to safety. But the trail remained open. The Communists stationed 75,000 people along the trail to keep it open. If one section was blocked, they simply hacked another path through the jungle nearby.

Thousands of tons of supplies were manhandled down the Ho Chi Minh Trail on bicycles. A pack bike could carry a 150-pound (70 kilogram) load, twice as much as a porter. When he had delivered his load, the porter rode back to pick up the next one.

Chemical Warfare

The United States was bitterly criticized at home and abroad when it was learned that U.S. planes were using poisonous chemicals to defoliate the jungle – strip the trees bare of leaves – to reveal tracks and hiding places. Powerful weed killers, including one called Agent Orange, were sprayed over the jungle. Napalm bombs that burned the foliage were also dropped. These deadly chemicals killed or disfigured soldiers and civilians alike.

LISTENING IN

The Americans developed devices to pinpoint enemy movements by night. Battery-powered sensors dropped by U.S. planes planted themselves on the jungle floor. They radioed back information to U.S. listening posts.

Helicopters played a key part in American tactics. Only when the Communists used Russian Sam-17 ground-to-air missiles from 1972 onward did they become vulnerable.

Stalemate

In 1967 nearly one-and-a-half million men were engaged in the war. The U.S. forces had grown to nearly half a million, and their numbers were still rising.

By the late 1960s, over 5,000 U.S. helicopters were operating in Vietnam, transporting men and arms swiftly over the treacherous jungle below. This rapid mobility won many victories for the Americans, but not control of the countryside. When fighting was over, the helicopters took the U.S. troops back to their bases, and the Communists returned to take the land.

HELICOPTERS AT WAR

The first helicopters to reach Vietnam, in 1961, were intended for quick transport of key supplies. They were soon put to more and more uses, as their value in battle was recognized. New types were produced for a multitude of different purposes.

Large models could transport an entire base of prefabricated buildings, with its defenses, weapons and equipment, deep into enemy territory, or pick up damaged aircraft and bring them back for repair.

Troop-carrying helicopters, able to airlift a whole division of 15,000 men within hours, were escorted by heavily armed helicopter gunships.

Specialized units called Medevacs flew in helicopters to lift nearly 170,000 casualties from the scene of battle.

A soldier of the North Vietnamese army. His weapons and equipment were simple and cheap – at least at the start of the war. This soldier has the basic Soviet AK47 rifle and a Soviet-made antitank missile launcher. A cloth tube looped around him was stuffed with enough food for seven days.

Sitting it Out

The Communists knew that they could not repeat the kind of victory they had won against the French at Dien Bien Phu. The U.S. forces were too large and well armed for that. They were confident that the American public would not stand for a long drawn out war and in the end would force their government to bring the U.S. troops home.

Americans at home could not understand what was going on. Television showed pictures of war in every U.S. home. There were terrible stories of U.S. troops killing innocent civilians. Planes regularly brought back bodies of U.S. servicemen killed in a war that seemed to have no end. Young men drafted into the army were increasingly reluctant to fight in a war that meant little or nothing to them, or to which they were opposed.

Morale in the services began to fall. Yet, as 1967 ended, U.S. troops and their South Vietnamese allies won several major victories. General Westmoreland was able to tell President Johnson and the public that at last their side was making real progress in the war.

The American public lost faith in President Johnson as a result of the Tet Offensive. They believed he had not told them the truth about the war. On March 31, 1968, Johnson announced that he would not seek re-election as president later that year. At the same time he cut back the bombing of North Vietnam. In May he began peace talks in Paris with the North Vietnamese.

The Tet Offensive

By 1968 the Americans and the South Vietnamese army were winning most of their encounters with the Communists. At a famous 1967 press conference General Westmoreland had announced "the end begins to come into view." The American people began to believe that the war was as good as won.

The Communists were losing so many men that they began to doubt whether they could carry on much longer. To end the war quickly, General Giap planned a massive surprise offensive against the cities of the South.

The Vietnamese mark their New Year with several days of celebration. It is called the Tet festival and, in the past, both sides had stopped fighting at that time. But in early 1968, however, General Giap ordered his forces to attack as Tet began at the end of January.

More than 80,000 Communists took part in assaults on over 100 targets. Their main attack was on Saigon where they captured the U.S. embassy. The Americans fought back quickly. Within a week, they drove the Communists out of most of the cities and the Communists suffered huge losses. The Viet Cong sustained 30,000 casualties.

Victory or Defeat?
Although Tet was an American victory, the American people were shocked and appalled by it. How could a "beaten enemy" have mounted the most savage assault of the whole conflict? Public opinion turned against President Johnson and the military commanders. Americans wanted the United States out of a war they could not win. The Communist defeat had in effect become a Communist victory.

THE SIEGE OF KHE SANH

Khe Sanh is close to the Ho Chi Minh Trail. The U.S. Army set up a base there to stop supplies coming down the trail from reaching Communist forces in South Vietnam. Ten days before the Tet Offensive began, a force of 15,000 Communists launched an attack on the 5,000 U.S. and South Vietnamese troops holding the base.

Khe Sanh was surrounded. All supplies to the base had to be flown in and dropped by parachute. The siege lasted for 77 days before U.S. ground troops fought their way through to the base.

During the siege the U.S. Air Force dropped 100,000 bombs on the enemy. Khe Sanh became the most heavily bombed place in history.

Phantom fighter bombers strike at the Communist forces besieging Khe Sanh.

America Votes for Peace

MY LAI

Nothing in the whole war shocked the American people more than the story of My Lai. In March 1968 U.S. soldiers had landed by helicopter near the small village of My Lai. They had expected to trap Viet Cong, but found only women and children, and old men. The soldiers were bewildered and afraid. The Viet Cong had surprised and ambushed them before. Now, alone in the jungle, they became panic-stricken and turned on My Lai. They burned it down and methodically slaughtered nearly 500 villagers. The news got out, and an inquiry into the massacre dragged on until 1971. The killings sickened America and became a powerful argument for getting out of the war.

The thoughts of the American people were united in one idea – how to make peace and pull out of Vietnam. They elected Richard Nixon as their President, with the task of getting the United States out of the war. Nixon called his policy "Vietnamization." American troops were to be gradually withdrawn, while the South Vietnamese Army was trained and equipped to replace them. The withdrawal began in July 1969 with 25,000 troops. Later in the year Nixon announced that a further 85,000 would follow. Meanwhile, in Paris, the peace talks dragged on. They were to continue through 1970, into 1971, and on into 1972 with no agreement in sight.

More Fighting, More Protest

In 1970 the war spread to Cambodia, where the North Vietnamese had crossed the border and set up military bases. The Cambodians appealed for help to drive out the invaders. The Americans responded, first with air support and then, in April, by sending in ground troops.

This widening of the war raised a storm of protest in America. Students demonstrated in over 400 colleges across the nation. In May, 100,000 protesters packed the streets of Washington to call for an end to the war. Nixon gave way to public opinion. In June, U.S. troops withdrew from Cambodia.

Meanwhile the run-down of American forces in South Vietnam was continuing. The North watched and saw the chance of a quick victory. In the spring of 1972, they invaded the South. The South Vietnamese fought back with unusual stubbornness and, with massive U.S. air support, checked the Communist advance. The battle died down, so Nixon called off the air force. But the North attacked again. This time the Americans hit back with an air bombardment so heavy and sustained that it threatened total destruction of North Vietnam's economy and forced them to stop fighting.

The air attacks on the North ended on December 30, 1972, and peace talks began again. On January 27, 1973, Henry Kissinger, the American negotiator, signed an agreement with North Vietnam that ended the conflict and provided for the release of prisoners of war.

A Communist soldier waves the North Vietnamese flag in triumph over a captured bunker in South Vietnam.

Victory to the North

The last U.S. combat troops left South Vietnam in March 1973, two months after the cease-fire was signed. But the agreement allowed 150,000 Communist soldiers to stay in the country and the South Vietnamese were unable to drive them out. American aid was dwindling, while Soviet help for the North had grown considerably. Fighting continued all through 1973 and 1974, showing how weak the South Vietnamese forces had become. On August 8, 1974, President Nixon resigned and Vice President Gerald Ford took his place. No one could tell whether the new president would continue to support South Vietnam. This uncertainty encouraged the Communists to risk a final assault. In January 1975, North Vietnam began a full-scale general offensive against the South.

The Last Days of South Vietnam

The cease-fire agreement permitted the Americans to give the South Vietnamese air support if attacked, but their help was halfhearted. The North Vietnamese pushed steadily southward. People who had opposed the Communists fled in terror before their advance. They jammed the roads leading south. Along the coast, swarms of little boats pushed off, awash with frantic refugees. In Saigon, U.S. helicopters flew 8,000 of their South Vietnamese supporters to safety aboard American warships anchored offshore. The last guards at the American embassy were airlifted off the roof as looters broke down the main door. On April 30, the North Vietnamese army captured Saigon. The Communist victory was complete.

Tens of thousands of South Vietnamese fled before the advancing Communists in what was later called "The Convoy of Tears."

The Continuing Conflict

The Communists lost no time in taking over South Vietnam. Communists occupied every position in government. Saigon was renamed Ho Chi Minh City. In 1976 North and South Vietnam were united to form the single nation of Vietnam. Hanoi became the capital.

The Terrible Cost of War
Well over a million North and South Vietnamese were killed. About 58,000 Americans died. The war injured and disabled hundreds of thousands of people in mind and body. Ten million fled their homes and became refugees. Much of Vietnam was ruined. American bombing smashed most of North Vietnam's industries and wrecked its cities, roads, and railroads. South Vietnam suffered worst of all, because most of the fighting had taken place there. Furthermore, the chemicals dropped by the Americans may have done permanent harm to the environment.

New Conflicts
A few days before the fall of Saigon, Communists known as the Khmer Rouge seized power in Cambodia. Led by Pol Pot, they renamed the country Kampuchea. The Khmer Rouge were backed by China and were hostile to the Vietnamese Communists. Trouble broke out on the border between the two countries. In 1978 Vietnam invaded Kampuchea, defeated the Khmer Rouge and replaced Pol Pot's government with a pro-Vietnamese government. Pol Pot and his Khmer followers retreated into Kampuchea's thick jungles and, supplied by their Chinese allies, waged a guerrilla war against the Vietnamese and their supporters.

Right: This map of Indochina shows Vietnam's two battle fronts after the war in Vietnam was over.

Below: In 1979 the Chinese army invaded Vietnam, but it lacked recent experience of combat, (it had last fought in Korea in 1953). Compared with the Vietnamese forces, Chinese tactics were as out of date as these T-59 tanks.

An Old Enemy

The Chinese were embarrassed and angered by the Vietnamese defeat of Pol Pot and his Khmer Rouge. So China announced that it would teach Vietnam a lesson. In 1979, 80,000 Chinese troops invaded Vietnam. The Russian-armed Vietnamese army fought back so fiercely that the Chinese were compelled to rush in extra troops, until 200,000 were engaged. The fighting ended when the Chinese withdrew their forces. They destroyed several towns and burned crops in the fields to punish the Vietnamese.

CHINA

HONG KONG

Hanoi

LAOS

Gulf of Tonkin

Hainan

Vientiane

THAILAND

VIETNAM

South China Sea

Mekong R.

CAMBODIA

Phnom Penh

Ho Chi Minh City (Saigon)

inese
etnamese

Boat People

The Fruits of War

The consequences of the Vietnam War have continued to be felt long after the war ended. The war was the longest ever fought by the United States. It was also the first foreign war in which American troops did not accomplish what they had set out to do. Opinion is still divided about whether or not the war should have been fought and whether or not it could have been won.

The Vietnam "Vets"

The returning troops were not always welcomed as heroes. Many felt hurt and angry that the nation did not understand, or care about, the sacrifices they had made by fighting in Vietnam. Some could not adjust to civilian life. Cases of drug abuse, divorce, and suicide are relatively common among Vietnam Veterans. Others cannot hold down jobs. Some have turned to violent crime.

Misery and Despair in Vietnam

The North Vietnamese began to compel the South to accept the Communist system immediately after the fighting ended. Hundreds of thousands of South Vietnamese were forced into "re-education centers," which were in fact concentration camps of the most brutal kind. Huge numbers of terrified families fled by sea in whatever boats they could lay their hands on, hoping to find sanctuary abroad. Thousands of these "boat people" drowned. Others were murdered by pirates. The flow of political refugees has now ceased, but the boat people keep on coming. Those who flee now seek a more prosperous life overseas. For Vietnam remains a desperately poor country, shattered by half a century of war.

Fearing for their lives, South Vietnamese refugees took to the sea. In the immediate aftermath, some were picked up by U.S. Navy vessels, but many were drowned as their overladen craft went down. Others made it to the Philippines, Thailand or Hong Kong. Today the refugees still set out but those that make it ashore in neighboring countries are usually unwelcome.

Ngo Dinh Diem 1901-63
Leader of South Vietnam
from 1954. His harsh rule
made him hated, and in 1963
he was overthrown and shot
by a group of army generals.

William Westmoreland 1914-
General who commanded
American forces in
Indochina from 1964-1968,
during the hardest fighting of
the Vietnam War.

Richard Nixon 1913-
United States President
1969-1974. He promised to
end America's part in the
Vietnam War. The last U.S.
combat troops left Vietnam
during his presidency.

Important People and Events of the War

1954
May 7 Vietminh capture Dien
Bien Phu. French rule in
Vietnam ends.
July Vietnam divided into two
states by the Great Powers at
the Geneva Conference.
1956
April 21 United States takes
over the training of South
Vietnamese armed forces.
1957
Viet Cong began armed
resistance against Diem's
South Vietnamese
government.
1959
Ho Chi Minh orders
construction of Ho Chi Minh
Trail.

1961
September The first Viet Cong
attacks in South Vietnam.
Nov. 16 President Kennedy
announces increased U.S.
military aid to South Vietnam.
1962
More than 4,000 U.S. military
advisers working in South
Vietnam. Viet Cong control
large areas of South Vietnam.
1963
Nov. 1-2 President Diem
overthrown and killed.
Nov. 22 President Kennedy
assassinated. Lyndon Johnson
succeeds him.
1964
July 30 Gulf of Tonkin
incident. Johnson granted

power by Congress "to take all
necessary measures to repel
any armed attack" and to
"prevent further aggression."
1965
March 2 Operation Rolling
Thunder begins.
March 6 U.S. Marines sent to
Da Nang, the first U.S. ground
troops to enter the war.
Nov. Widespread antiwar
protests in America.
1966-67
American forces in South
Vietnam continue to grow.
1968
Jan.22-April 7 Siege of Khe
Sanh.
Jan. 30-late Feb. Tet Offensive.
March 16 My Lai Massacre.

Henry Kissinger 1923-
Chief U.S. negotiator at the four-year-long peace talks in Paris. They ended in 1973 and the last American troops left Vietnam soon afterward.

March 31 Rolling Thunder ends.
May 13 Paris peace talks begin.
Nov. Richard Nixon elected U.S. President.
Dec. Half a million U.S. troops now in South Vietnam.
1969
June 8 Nixon announces that U.S. troops will begin to leave Vietnam.
Sept. 4 Ho Chi Minh dies.
1970
Anti-war movement in America grows.
May Huge protest meeting in Washington.
Dec. U.S. strength in South Vietnam down to 335,800.
1971
Paris peace talks drag on
Dec. Heavy U.S. air attacks on North Vietnam.
1972
March 30 North Vietnamese

Gerald Ford 1913-
United States President from 1974 when Richard Nixon resigned in disgrace. He continued Nixon's policy of getting America out of the conflict in Indochina.

invade South Vietnam.
Aug. 12 Last U.S. combat ground troops leave South Vietnam.
Dec. 18 Massive U.S. air attacks on North Vietnam.
Dec 30 North Vietnamese agree to a truce. U.S. bombing ceases.
1973
Jan. 27 In Paris, North Vietnam and South Vietnam, the United States and the Viet Cong sign a cease-fire agreement.
March 29 Last U.S. ground troops leave Vietnam.
1974
Aug. 8 Gerald Ford succeeds Richard Nixon as U.S. President.
1975
April 17 Khmer Rouge led by Pol Pot seize power in Cambodia.

Pol Pot 1925-
Communist ruler of Cambodia (which he renamed Kampuchea) from 1975-1978. During his brief rule of terror, millions died from overwork and starvation or by execution.

April 30 North Vietnamese capture Saigon. South Vietnam surrenders and Vietnam becomes one country. Huge numbers of boat people flee to find refuge abroad.
1978
Vietnam invades Cambodia (Kampuchea).
1979
Vietnam defeat the Khmer Rouge in Kampuchea. Pot Pol takes refuge in the jungle.
Feb. 19 Chinese invade Vietnam "as a punishment."
March Chinese withdraw from Vietnam.
1989
Sept. Vietnamese army leaves Cambodia (Kampuchea.)
Dec. Hong Kong returns 51 boat people to Vietnam.
1990
U.S. and Vietnam start normalization process.

Index

Agent Orange 17
Aircraft 7, 10, 11, 14-17, 19
Aircraft carriers 10, 11
Americans *See* United States
Antiaircraft guns 7, 14, 18

B-52 bombers 14, 15
Bicycles 16
Boat people 25, 27, 28, 31
Bombing 7, 9, 11, 14-16, 20, 21, 23, 26, 31
Booby traps 12, 13
Bridges 14, 16

Cambodia 5 (map), 16, 22, 26, 27
Casualties 14, 19, 26
Ceasefire 24, 25, 31
Chemical warfare 17, 26
China 6
Chinese 4, 6, 26, 27, 31
Cities 14, 26
Communists 5, 6, 8, 11, 14, 16, 18-20, 22, 24-26
Conscription 10

Da Nang 8, 30
Diem, President *See* Ngo Dinh Diem
Dien Bien Phu 6, 7, 19, 30
Doves and hawks 14
Draft 10

Europe 6

Farmers 4
Ford, President Gerald 24, 31
France 4, 6
French 4-6, 8, 17, 19

Geneva 8, 30
Giap, General *See* Vo Nguyen Giap
Guam 14
Guerrilla warfare 6, 8, 12, 13, 26
Guns 7

Haiphong 10
Hanoi 4, 6, 26, 27
Hawks and doves 14
Helicopter 9, 11, 18, 19, 25
Ho Chi Minh 5, 6, 8, 12, 30, 31

Ho Chi Minh City 6, 26, 27 *See also* Saigon
Ho Chi Minh Trail 16

Indochina 4, 6, 16, 31
Industries 26

Japan 6
Johnson, President Lyndon B. 8, 9, 11, 19, 20, 30
Jungles 6, 11, 12, 13, 16-18, 26

Kampuchea 26, 31 *See also* Cambodia
Kennedy, President John F. 8, 9, 30
Khe Sanh 21, 30
Khmer Rouge 26, 27, 31
Kissinger, Henry 23, 31
Korean War 10, 26

Laos 5 (map), 16, 27 (map)
Listening devices 17

Mao Tse-Tung 6, 12
Mekong River 5, 27 (map)
My Lai 22, 30

Napalm 17
Navarre, General Henri, 6, 7
Ngo Dinh Diem 5, 8, 30
Nguyen Van Thanh *See* Ho Chi Minh
Nixon, President Richard 22, 24, 30, 31
North Vietnam/Vietnamese 5, 8, 9, 14, 16, 19, 20, 22-26, 28, 31
North Vietnamese army 6, 7, 8, 19, 25 *See also* Communists; Vietminh

Paddy fields 4, 11
Paris peace talks 19, 22, 31
Peace agreement 23
Phantom fighter bombers 21
Phnom Penh 27 (map)
Pol Pot 26, 27, 31
Protests 23, 30, 31
Public opinion 14, 16, 17, 19, 20, 22, 23, 28

Railroads 4, 14, 26

Red River 5
Refugees 25, 26, 28
Rice fields 4, 6, 12
Roads 4, 14, 16, 26
Rolling Thunder 14, 30, 31

Saigon 6, 11, 20, 25, 26
Smart bombs 14
South Vietnam/Vietnamese 5, 8-11, 14, 16, 19-22, 25-28, 30
South Vietnamese army 8, 20-22, 24
South Vietnamese government 8, 12, 14
Southeast Asia 4, 11, 14
Soviet aircraft 14
Sugar 4

T-59 tanks 26
Television 19
Tet Offensive 20, 21, 30
Tonkin, Gulf of 9, 27 (map), 30
Torpedo boats 9
Tunnels 13

United States (Americans) 8-14, 17-26, 28, 30, 31

Veterans 28
Vientiane 27 (map)
Viet Cong 8, 9, 11-14, 20, 22, 30
Vietminh 6, 7, 30
Vietnam 4 (map), 5 (map), 26, 27 (map), *See also* North Vietnam; South Vietnam
Vo Nguyen Giap 6, 7, 12, 20

Westmoreland, General William 14, 19, 20, 30
Withdrawal 22, 24
World War II 6